Airstreams:

Custom Interiors

Airstreams:

Custom Interiors

David Winick

Schiffer Publishing Ltd

4880 Lower Valley Road · Atglen, Pennsylvania 19310

Other Schiffer Books on Related Subjects:
Small Space Living. Christine Brun. ISBN: 9780764331923. $34.99.

Schiffer Books are available at special discounts for bulk purchases for sales promotions or premiums. Special editions, including personalized covers, corporate imprints, and excerpts can be created in large quantities for special needs. For more information contact the publisher:

Published by Schiffer Publishing Ltd.
4880 Lower Valley Road
Atglen, PA 19310
Phone: (610) 593-1777; Fax: (610) 593-2002
E-mail: Info@schifferbooks.com

For the largest selection of fine reference books on this and related subjects, please visit our web site at
www.schifferbooks.com
We are always looking for people to write books on new and related subjects. If you have an idea for a book please contact us at the above address.

This book may be purchased from the publisher.
Include $5.00 for shipping.
Please try your bookstore first.
You may write for a free catalog.

In Europe, Schiffer books are distributed by
Bushwood Books
6 Marksbury Ave.
Kew Gardens
Surrey TW9 4JF England
Phone: 44 (0) 20 8392 8585; Fax: 44 (0) 20 8392 9876
E-mail: info@bushwoodbooks.co.uk
Website: www.bushwoodbooks.co.uk

Type set in Din/New Baskerville BT

ISBN: 978-0-7643-3539-6
Printed in China

Dedication

This book is dedicated to my daughter, Rebecca, who rose to an almost insurmountable challenge in her life.

No one could be prouder.

Foreword

The connection between Airstream the company and the universe of Airstream owners and enthusiasts has always been diverse, challenging, and a tremendous source of inspiration for those of us here in Jackson Center. We remain endlessly fascinated by the creativity we see applied to our products; both in how they are used and the redesigns people execute to make their Airstream unique and truly custom. Almost since the first aluminum trailer was produced in 1936, people have been applying their creative talents and craftsmanship to re-envision the product, often in surprising ways that tweak our assumptions. It's interesting to note that, while the Airstream shape has achieved the status of untouchable icon, the travel trailer interiors are regarded as a clean slate, a vessel, in a very real sense, for personal expression. Whether it's the trailers remade as rolling kitchens (many), mobile retail spaces (several), or Pam Anderson's Lovestream (one-of-a-kind), the iconic shape seems to invite all manner of tinkering.

But our favorites remain those that stay true to their original purpose: a home on wheels, with all (or many) of the conveniences needed to make a life (or weekend) on the road something to be cherished and enjoyed. In these we find amazement and delight, and thought-provoking approaches to solving the same design issues we confront daily. In our experience David Winick is one of the best, a nice balance of fresh takes and superb craftsmanship. Herein lie examples of his work for all to enjoy.

Bob Wheeler, President &
CEO Airstream, Inc.

Preface

David Winick has such a fine sense of the romance of post-war travel in this country. He combines modern sensitivities and hipness with the wide-eyed spirit of adventure that characterized an era of expansion. One can almost smell the powerful aromas of summer in his work; lemonade, varnished woods, coconut suntan oil, matches lighting charcoal…the ideals of a bygone era, refreshed again from our subconscious.

The romance of domestic travel, following the by-ways and highways across diverse geography to explore this country, is so fundamental to the American dream, and is well captured in Winick's work. His craftsmanship, keen eye for just the right combinations of materials, and his ability to maintain a consistent design language really sets his work apart, honoring the riveted aluminum badge. The materials he selects express the innocence of the 1950s and '60s.

Tin can tourists everywhere can envy the lovely softly glowing silver, rich woods, camp-chic patterns and colors with which he paints. David manages to reach down and grab those memories within us all, fondly recalling family vacations, bringing out the child in each of us. We are transported to a folding canvas chair, beneath a colorful striped awning, like a scene out of *LIFE* magazine.

Stewart Reed, Transportation Design Chair, Art Center College of Design, Pasadena

Acknowledgments

The arts are an integral component in my life, and my inspiration comes from family, friends, and peers, without whom this book would not be possible. It's these interconnections and relationships that give the soul and meaning to what I attempt to create. One doesn't instantly learn to build and design. It comes from the guidance and reinforcement of those whom have touched my life. To this end, I owe all a great debt.

Special thanks to my multi-talented daughter, Rebecca, and her wonderful family, Thom, Samantha, and Veronica. Gregg Palazzolo, my buddy and one of the most talented people I know, who provided advice, criticism, and some images for this book. Thanks man.

Thanks to Bob Wheeler, CEO and President of Airstream® Inc., Stewart Reed, Transportation Design Chair, Art Center College of Design, Pasadena and Dale "Pee Wee" Schwamborn, an international Airstream treasure, for honoring me by all contributing to this book.

In addition, I'd like to acknowledge Chris Cobb of the Forbo® Corporation, Steve Hingtgen of Vintage Trailer Supply, Imtra® Marine Products, US distributor for Fynspray hand pumps, Marti Domyancic, Progressive Dynamics® Inc., Moonshine Lamp and Shade, Zinger Sheet Metal, and Durant Custom Upholstery.

Additional imagery generously provided by Airstream Inc., Kathy McGrath, John Getz, Gregg Palazzolo, and Rebecca Gohl.

I would also like to offer a special acknowledgment to the growing legion of Airstream enthusiasts across the US and abroad, many whom I've come to know over the last several years.

"See More, *Live* More, Do More" –Wally Byam

Contents

Foreword
Preface
Acknowledgments

Introduction ...10

Chapter One: 1968 Airstream Caravel ...12

Chapter Two: Airstream's 75th Anniversary Limited Edition Bambi ...30

Chapter Three: 1950 Airstream Flying Cloud ...68

Chapter Four: 1948 Airstream Wee Wind ...94

Chapter Five: 1957 Airstream "18 Footer" ...120

Future Projects ...142
Afterword ...143
Resources ...144

Introduction

Few shapes on the road are as instantly recognizable and inspire as much passion as the Airstream trailer. Many Airstream owners share very similar qualities with the owners of that other American design icon, the Harley Davidson®. Both fraternities have exceptional loyalty to the brand; many have lifestyles that revolve around their rigs and bikes. Many individuals in both groups tattoo images of trailers and bikes on their bodies. Care and maintenance can border on the obsessive. They also share the common desire to get on the open road and explore. Stop wherever and whenever you feel like with no time restraints or reservations. They are modern day gypsies.

My first encounter with Airstream trailers took place when I was on a trip out West as a kid. I was seven years old. At the time, we had a 1956 Pontiac Safari station wagon. A Safari was the length of a limousine. It sported rounded stubby tailfins, mountains of chrome, yards of stainless steel trim, and enough doodads to satisfy an Arab Sheik. This was back in an era when machines and devices were built to last and cars were made of metal and not plastic. America was king of industry. Japan's major export was a transistor radio with the sound quality of speaking into an empty soup can. That Pontiac was so beefy that if you added a gun turret you could have driven it into battle. It was painted a complementary two-tone jungle-green metallic with a cream-colored roof and grainy white leather upholstery, which my mother hated for obvious reasons. One of its many unique features was a rear facing flip up seat in the back with an enormous panoramic rear power window. This was a selling point as far as my parents were concerned. The further from the front my parents put me and my cousin, Bernie, the better for the sake of their sanity. We were always play fighting and making noise.

During one of the lulls in a wrestling match I was watching the cars and trucks pass by on the other side of Route 66 when, traveling in the opposite direction, an Airstream trailer being pulled by a Chevy convertible whizzed by. I had no idea what it was at the time but the image stuck with me. It was the coolest shape I'd ever seen on wheels. And if it interrupted a wrestling event with Bernie, it had to be.

That experience stayed with me. I didn't think of it again for many years … until the day I saw one for sale sitting in a parking lot near a mall. I pulled in and stopped. It was unlocked and I was able to look inside. At the time I was in my 20s, nearly broke, and in design school. Again I filed away the experience. It wasn't until a few years ago that I again came in contact with an Airstream. That sealed the deal. I was at a point where I could buy one. That was the beginning step to what I'm doing now: Building custom Airstream travel trailers. I also didn't anticipate that I'd become an Airstream designer. I've been told many times during my life that if you're passionate about something you will find a way to do it—and be successful. Thanks for the great advice mom and dad.

I bought my first Airstream sight unseen on Ebay. There were lots of images, but I really didn't know what questions to ask. I didn't know much other than it was really cool, seemed to be in great shape, and I wanted it. Sound familiar? That was some time ago and many trailers. I optimistically drove out to the West Coast to pick it up. I live in Michigan. It was a great road trip. I was lucky. The seller represented it honestly. That Caravel was a nice trailer. Damn nice. I could hardly wait to begin the camping trip home. I used it as-is for about a year. Then one day in early winter I thought I'd do a little work to it. I have a design studio with metal and woodworking facilities. So during a lull in projects in my shop, I backed the trailer into a bay. Well, one thing led to another and I totally disassembled the interior. I just couldn't leave it alone. I began to rebuild it as I felt it should look. I figured that if I liked it, someone else would too. I've learned to go with my gut feelings. I've worked in the design field for many years as a set and prop designer and as art director for feature films and photography. I have also been fabricating decorative architectural metal work and commissions for bars, nightclubs, and commercial businesses. I've worked with and am familiar with many different materials. Rebuilding the Caravel gave me a great feeling. When I finally decided to sell that Caravel, it sold in less than a week when I listed it on my website.

That was the beginning. I now build and design trailers for customers all over the US and abroad. This book's primary focus is on the interiors. I enjoy the challenge of working with confined spaces. Plus, there is something compelling about the Airstream shape. If you own an Airstream you may know what I'm talking about. And if you own more than one, I'm preaching to the choir. If you're reading this book and don't have one, I predict that you may start daydreaming about them. It doesn't go away. Ask me. I know.

This book is a collection of five new and vintage Airstream trailers that have been designed and fabricated in my studio. Some of you may be interested in only images while others may desire detailed narrative. I've endeavored to strike a balance for everyone. I hope that you have as much fun reading this book as I had in my studio building and photographing these trailers. Here's to fun, travel, adventure, and the anticipation of what may be around the next corner. Saddle up.

Chapter One:

1968 Airstream Caravel

A 1968 Caravel with a beautiful original exterior free of dents and blemishes.

Inspiration comes in many forms. In May 2004, a conversation with a friend turned to small living spaces and the subject of trailers came up.

We both agreed that people don't need a lot of space and I'm drawn to the notion that less is more. As a designer, I find working with limited space very challenging and rewarding. I mentioned my long-standing attraction to Airstream trailers. I decided that I would learn more about them and began to research the history of the company and the various models. Up to this point, I knew virtually nothing about them other than I thought they were the coolest shapes. I couldn't wait to have one.

After doing much reading I felt that models before 1970 had much more charm that newer units. In my mission to find one, I began to haunt E-bay like a stalker. In mid-June, a 1968 Caravel was listed on E-bay. It's a small, relatively lightweight trailer that I thought would be a perfect trailer for road trips. I love the desert Southwest and spend a great deal of time in the Four Corners area. This would be ideal. The trailer appeared to be in great condition. I requested additional images of it and that cinched it. I bought it. The trailer was located in Morrow Bay, several hours north of Los Angeles. After driving across the country I brought it back to Michigan and used it for about a year before I

began to consider doing some slight modification to the interior. It also had some minor water damage to an area of the floor that I wanted to repair. I have a pretty large studio so I brought it inside and began to work on it. One thing led to another and I decided that I'd totally disassemble the interior. I decided to modify it to suit my taste. I had a blast. I had wanted to do this for ages. The process took approximately twelve weeks.

The 1968 Caravel is a very cool rig. It's a first cousin to the short-lived Bambi, which preceded it. Its modest size allows it to be towed with most trucks and SUVs. To me, it's on the waning side of the classic Airstream body styles. Airstreams evolved a few years later to a distinctive 1970s airplane look. Mostly it was the newly designed windows that gave the effect. The latter Caravel has a unique look as well. It's an underrated model. I prefer it to the Bambi. I think it's mostly the name "Bambi" that makes that model so popular. My all time favorite is the mid-50s Flying Cloud. It's a few feet longer than the Caravel. I see it as the definitive Airstream shape. In 1954. the Flying Cloud's rear end was changed from being vertical to a slight outward angle. To me, the addition was a huge improvement to an already classic form. There were many other changes too. It has a sister called the Caravanner, which is another one of my favorites.

Photo courtesy of Karen Getz

The trailer was in exceptionally good condition for a 40+ year old trailer, save for a few small areas of floor damage. It appeared that there was a small leak at the water pump that went unattended for a length of time. The original layout was very functional and I felt that there was no need to alter it significantly. I thought a mix of the original interior with modifications and embellishments was just the ticket.

The first order of business was removing the entire interior and components, including the wraparound fiberglass bath. I then removed the original tile floor and replaced the water-damaged sections of subfloor. During this process, all the aluminum interior wall panels were removed, leaving only the fiberglass front storage compartment and the fiberglass end cap in the rear bathroom. The old insulation was also tossed, leaving a tidy aluminum shell, which made rewiring for additional power needs a breeze.

After removing everything from the interior and repairing the floor, it was time to install new linoleum sheet. I'll be singing the praises of linoleum throughout the book. Great material and it's as green as a product can be. It's not for the faint-of-heart to install, however. It must be cut first to the exact outline of the space, which requires a template. It's not flexible like inexpensive vinyl flooring, which any hillbilly can install with a beer and a utility knife.

After the floor was installed, I wired, reinsulated, and then new mill-finish aluminum panels were pop-riveted into place. I decided to Zolotone® the fiberglass storage area over the dinette. Zolotone® is one of several companies that manufacture fleck paint. Think 1960s auto trunks. This stuff adheres to about anything it

contacts, is extremely durable, and hides defects and scratches. Older Airstreams interior walls were entirely painted in this manner. The original Caravel walls were clad in grainy beige vinyl covered aluminum, which was practical yet über boring—a nod to airplane cabin interiors of the same era. They went to the aluminum recycler. I'm not of a mind that original is better. Wally Byam, the founder of Airstream and a very forward thinking individual, always strived to make his trailers better. Not cheaper. In no way am I comparing myself to him. I'm just saying…

Plumbing was replaced and installed as well as the re-gelled fiberglass sink and bath surround. A high-end sound system was wired in and new cabinetry and countertop installed.

Front fiberglass compartment being prepped and painted with Zolotone®.

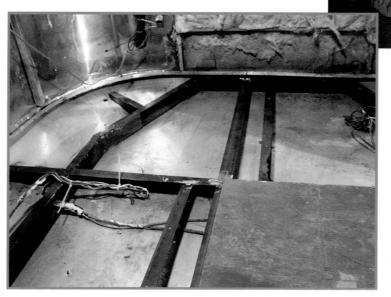

Removal of plywood subfloor and frame repair.

Prepping galley area for new wiring, plumbing, and cabinetry.

Close up of die cast aluminum Caravel badge.

Bath wall replacement with riveted and soldered copper sheet.

Rear view of the Caravel featuring galley and copper bath surround.

Dinette seat bases being reinstalled after refinishing. Fresh water tank inside false front between seat bases.

I used a bit of copper sheet in this trailer. The exhaust vent for the propane fridge is a flimsy piece of molded plastic, which over 40 years chemically degrades and becomes brittle. I made a template and fabricated a copper vent to replace it. In the bath, I made templates of the entire curved rear overhead fiberglass surround and covered the entire area with riveted copper sheet. Both areas then received several coats of protective finish. I'd like to do this again. I liked the results. It's a really cozy bath with a coppery glow. I also fabricated an exhaust fan from existing and new parts. I eliminated the cabinet over the stove. Its only purpose was to get in the way of my head. After I smacked my head a couple of times, it was on the list of things to delete. It also made the galley area feel less claustrophobic.

Copper exhaust duct for propane refrigerator.

Segmented copper panels on rear end cap.

Alpine subwoofer and
CDT 2-way speakers
[not shown].

Eclipse amplifier and receiver.

Installing copper in bathroom.

Now it was time to reinstall all new walnut cabinetry and appliances. That accomplished, drawings and templates were made for all the cushions and pillows and sent off to the upholsterer with some great knobby vintage-styled textiles.

I felt the end result was elegant but understated. Everyone who spent time in the trailer commented on the available space. This turned into a very cool Caravel.

I fabricated this exhaust vent from stainless steel, using the original fan motor.

Sink in rear bath area. I like the coppery glow.

Shelf for miscellaneous small containers and hooks for utensils.

Completed galley, although there are some final trim pieces to be installed.

21

The first time out camping in this trailer convinced me that I wanted to do a project like this again. I was hooked. I needed a way to do this full-time.

Enter the Airstream Corp.

Flip up counter extension. Adds additional counter when sitting at the dinette table.

Left: Glass holder and storage shelf that were fabricated for the galley.

A view of the finished galley area.

A view of the galley at entry door.

The current owners of the Caravel are John and Karen Getz.

"A talented photographer, metalworker, and designer, David is best known in the Airstream world as the creator of the "Home Sweet Home" screen door guard, and a uniquely refurbished 1968 Caravel. Both have earned him praise for his artistry, quality, and metalworking expertise. Operating as Winick Design Studio since 1992, David specialized in sets and props for film and TV projects. In recent years, he found time to indulge his long interest in Airstreams, and started on the Caravel project in his large metal and woodworking studio.

The Caravel, a frame-up rebuild completed in 2003 after eight weeks of effort, is a thing of beauty that has attracted attention from both vintage enthusiasts and the Airstream Factory designers."

Airstream Life Magazine [2005]

The current owners of the Caravel are John and Karen Getz.
Photo courtesy of Karen Getz

Powder coated rims.

"Home Sweet Home" stainless steel door guard that I designed for Airstreams from 1965 to the present.

The door guard designed for the 75th Anniversary Bambi which reads, "The Airstream Company, Jackson Center, Ohio."

The original steel LP tanks were replaced with 30# aluminum tanks.

Photo courtesy of Karen Getz

Chapter Two:

Airstream's 75th Anniversary Limited Edition Bambi

Designing Airstream's 75th anniversary Bambi was not on my to-do list in the summer of 2005. In fact, I had no idea that they were approaching their 75th year of operations. At the time I had recently finished the rebuilding of the 1968 Caravel and my business was not rebuilding/customizing Airstream trailers. It was more of a hobby.

That summer I was contacted by the editor of *Airstream Life* magazine and asked if I would be interested in photographing the Airstream International Rally, which was being held that year in Lansing, Michigan. Rich Luhr [the magazine's founder] had seen some of my photographs of trailers and liked my work. I agreed to go and set off for the rally with my little '68 Caravel in tow. During the course of the events over the weekend I was introduced to Dicky Riegel and Bob Wheeler. At the time, Dicky was Airstream's CEO and Bob was vice president of engineering as I recall. Since that time, Bob has become the CEO of the company. They had an opportunity to view the trailer that I had brought and they both were very enthusiastic about the interior. I asked them if they would consider my building twelve custom one-of-a-kind trailers with the notion that they would be collector trailers with the same feeling that the '68 Caravel had. Their reply was how about seventy-five? But they wanted their factory to build them and me to design it.

So a dialog began between us and we eventually signed a contract that following spring. We agreed that I would build the prototype in my studio in Michigan. We also chose to use the 19' Bambi platform and keep the basic electrical, plumbing, and propane systems in place to alleviate an entire change in the production line. I felt it was a great challenge and had them send me a top of the line 19' production Bambi so I could get a feel for its use of space. I had that trailer in my possession for a couple of months. I'd study the interior and evaluate its utility and function. I was not impressed. I felt there was definitely room for improvement in materials and use of space. I also wished to use more 'green' materials.

I began to remove components while I waited for the factory to build and deliver the shell in which I'd build the 'real' prototype. I'd make templates from drawings that I had sketched and began to change the placement of components and furniture. Then I'd make them out of plywood so I had an actual, physical, basic interior. By the time the shell arrived, I was confident that I had what I felt was a good solution that could be mass-produced. I felt that I solved the issue of the bathroom door only opening halfway before contacting the fixed mattress. I also improved on storage by at least double, and opened up the floor plan so two people would have more room to maneuver and feel less claustrophobic—which, in my opinion, was a real issue.

75th Anniversary Signature Bambi
Photo courtesy of Airstream Inc.

Building the mockup interior while deconstructing a production model at the studio before arrival of the prototype shell. This model had panoramic front windows, which the prototype shell would not have.

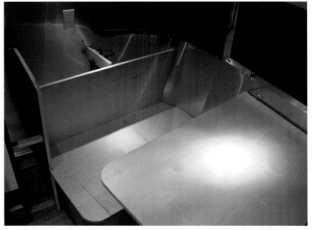

Checking fit of dinette mockup.

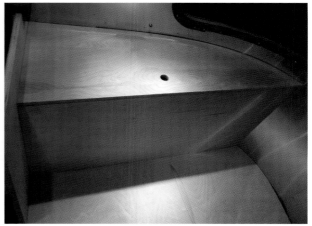

Mockup of dinette bulkhead storage.

Prototype shell fresh off the assembly line at the Airstream factory.

I wanted to use a porthole shaped window in the entry door and in the interior on the bathroom door. No modern Airstream had utilized that shape. I also wanted to allow as much light entry into the trailer as possible so we used fixed windows above and below the curbside operable side window. There were two small horizontal oval windows next to the galley, which I felt were worthless and seemed more like inoperable mail-slots. We deleted those and added an operable window, with fixed glass above. I had also wished to use aircraft grade aluminum on the exterior, but there were production issues and it would have added considerable cost to buff out 75 trailers to a mirror shine and clear coat them. Too bad. It would have been fantastic.

The prototype trailer arrives at the studio in Grand Rapids.

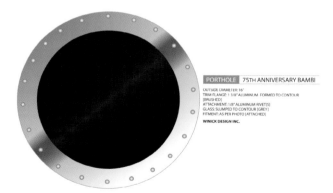

PORTHOLE 75TH ANNIVERSARY BAMBI

OUTSIDE DIAMETER: 16"
TRIM FLANGE: 1 3/8" ALUMINUM. FORMED TO CONTOUR [BRUSHED]
ATTACHMENT: 1/8" ALUMINUM RIVET[S]
GLASS: SLUMPED TO CONTOUR [GREY]
FITMENT: AS PER PHOTO [ATTACHED]
WINICK DESIGN INC.

Porthole design used in entry door and bath.

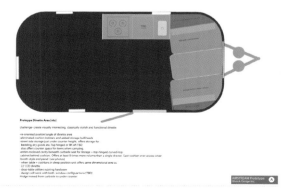

One of several initial floor-plans detailing dinette.

In the interior, my choice of flooring and surface material was linoleum. Good looking, extremely durable, and awarded the highest ratings of green products. The wood would be walnut plywood, curved and flat stock. All edgings and trim would be extruded aluminum with stainless steel fasteners. Designtex, the textile company I was working with, made a custom color way to contrast with a stock color that I chose for the upholstery and pillows. I also designed a pair of shades for the two sconces and a special stainless steel door-guard for the entry. I also tried to use every available space for some type of storage, while still allowing an open feel. It was my goal to have an interior that offered visual appeal, flexibility, durability, and function. And it needed to be fun.

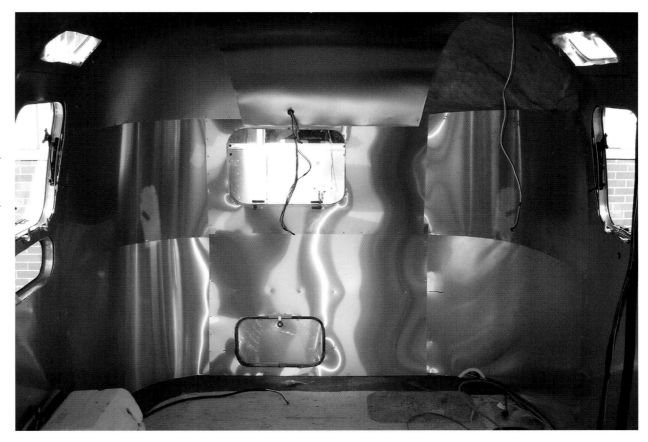

Prototype interior during "being buttoned up" process at the factory in Jackson Center.

Building the dinette in the prototype.

Installation of dinette.

Storage behind dinette seating.

Completed dinette seating with curved walnut base.

The completed
bathroom exterior.
Next, it was on to
installing the galley.

Prototype shell in the studio.

Checking fit of curbside seat base with curved storage top in open position.

Curbside dinette base.

Nearing completion of the dinette and galley.

There is plenty of additional storage behind the bulkheads.

A view of the finished galley and dinette.

Shelving components await assembly for shipment
to the Airstream factory.

75TH ANNIVERSARY EDITION

Continuing in the Airstream tradition of quality, innovation and design, Airstream is proud to introduce the 75th Anniversary Airstream Custom by designer David Winick.
The custom built 19ft Bambi was handmade with a vision for the rich heritage of a classic American icon.

Creating the 75th Anniversary trailer for an American icon has been great fun, and the results are a reflection of that spirit. Cheers and happy 75th!

-David Winick [Winick Design Studio]

75th anniversary edition promotion .

75TH ANNIVERSARY EDITION

Continuing in the Airstream tradition of quality, innovation and design, Airstream is proud to introduce the 75th Anniversary Airstream Custom by designer David Winick.
The custom built 19ft Bambi was handmade with a vision for the rich heritage of a classic American icon.

Creating the 75th Anniversary trailer for an American icon has been great fun, and the results are a reflection of that spirit. Cheers and happy 75th!

David Winick [Winick Design Studio]

Dickey Riegel and myself at the introduction of the
75th Anniversary Bambi in Louisville, KY. (2006)
Photo courtesy of Rebecca Gohl

75th anniversary edition signature badge.

75th anniversary edition prototype at the RVIA show in Louisville.

The build took approx four months in my studio. During that time, I updated Airstream via digital images so they knew where I was headed. They were remarkably flexible with what I wished to do. They set no parameters on the design.

I appreciated their trust and this project became a favorite of mine. It was four months of fun and lots of work.

Photo courtesy of Airstream Inc.

Completed dinette.

Curved walnut
lid behind seat
hinges forward for
additional storage.

Galley area and dinette.

View toward bedroom and bath

Wardrobe and bathroom.

Pull-out section can double as a table when laying on the sofa.

Converted with extension and cushions to bed position.

Rear storage with additional storage under the bed via an access panel.

Flat screen TV and
CD/DVD player.

CD and DVD player above flat screen TV.

Convertible L-shaped lounge.

Curved ply hinged to offer a storage nook. Panel hinged under sofa/bed for additional storage. Lift off panel under rear cushion to access more storage.

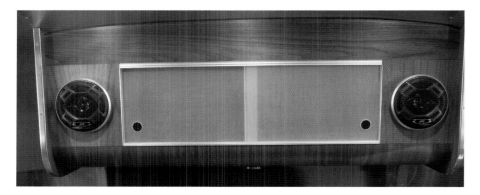

Storage locker over dinette.

Aluminum galley with furnace below.

Custom sconce, storage shelf with aluminum rail,
indexed for four glasses.

Aluminum galley with furnace below.

Wardrobe between bathroom and galley.

Shelf in galley for salt and pepper, etc., with
some handy chrome hooks.

Custom made sconce shades made for this production run.

One of the best compliments comes from purchasers of the 75 trailers who have set up owner registries to keep tabs on who has what sequentially numbered edition. I've also enjoyed the many emails and telephone calls since production. I designed this trailer for people. And if the owners are happy, I feel that I have been successful.

"It's like a SoHo loft, but mobile. Park this on the beach, catch a fish a day, and you're set."
Steve McCallion/Ziba Design

"Winick's design is an interesting combination of the richness of first-class railway cars combined with a distinct nautical flavor, thanks to the round porthole windows and vents. I find something incredibly alluring in the rich 'metal and wood' look and this glistening camper evokes a powerful emotional response.
The Anniversary model is based on Airstream's 19-foot Bambi trailer and sports a list price of just over $60,000. Winick tells me that he spent many years designing sets and props for film and photography and is intrigued by mid-century modern design. His passion for classic design is obvious, he managed to successfully combine beautiful aluminum curves, rich wood veneers, upholstery that's reminiscent of the 1940s, along with an ultra-modern flat screen television. The final result is almost enough to make me want to live in my driveway."
James Grahame/retrothing.com

"Airstream debuted a special 75th anniversary edition, 19-foot trailer that is cute beyond cute. Oh my goodness, I want one!"
Chuck Woodbury - Editor RV Travel.com

"Home Sweet Home" aftermarket custom door-guard designed by my studio. *Photo courtesy of David McGrath (campadk.com)*

"Home Sweet Home." The first door guard I designed for late model Airstreams. The door guard on the 75th anniversary Bambi was specifically designed for that model and it proved very popular with owners with other models.

Custom door-guard for 75th anniversary production. *Photo courtesy of Airstream Inc.*

Photo courtesy of Airstream Inc.

Kathy McGrath relaxing dockside with their 75th Anniversary Bambi in the background.
Photo courtesy of David McGrath (campadk.com)

David and Kathy McGrath's Bambi at Camp ADK.
Photo courtesy of David McGrath (campadk.com)

Photo courtesy of David McGrath (campadk.com)

Photo courtesy of David McGrath (campadk.com)

Chapter Three:

1950 Airstream Flying Cloud

A couple of summers ago the phone rang and on the other end was Bob Wheeler, Airstream Corp's President & CEO. He told me he had recently purchased a 1950 Flying Cloud. He said that I was the only person to build it for him and asked if I was interested in taking on the project. I accepted immediately. The trailer was going to be used by him and his family. Bob has given me a lot of leeway with what I felt was 'right' in a trailer when I designed the 75th Anniversary Bambi and this time was no exception. This was going to be the beginning of a great project.

The trailer was in very poor condition and was going to require a lot of work to get it to a neutral place so I could begin to work on the interior. Like the 1948 Wee Wind covered in this book, it also had the same deficient pipe frame chassis that all early Airstreams had. So step number one was to remove the trailer from the body and put a new frame under it. Since the trailer was at the Airstream factory in Jackson Center, Ohio, it was logical that the factory service department tackle this part of the project and get it roadworthy. While this was underway I drove to Ohio and Bob and I discussed his needs

and we taped off areas of the trailer to give us an idea of the basic layout. There wasn't any room for a shower in this unit and barely enough to accommodate a bathroom. This was due to the window placement. I also wanted to check out what was left of the original interior components and determine what was salvageable. As it was, I ended up reusing three aluminum overhead lockers. That was it. Everything else was too rusted, broken or rotten to be of any interest.

When the trailer was reunited with a new frame and axle, I returned to the factory and brought the Flying Cloud back to my studio in Michigan. I had a pretty good idea of what I was going to do and I began to fabricate a mockup of the interior with plywood. This trailer needed to have an element of fun with understated elegance. I wanted to keep the interior as open as I could, yet have plenty of storage and ample room for a bed. Since this model has a 'liner' rear end, it has a more severe curve and a bit less room. We wanted to make the bed a wide as could practically be done. There wasn't any extra room. The layout had to be planned to the inch.

The finished Flying Cloud in the sun for the first time in a few months.

With new systems in place, end caps polished, and electric routed in the walls, it's time to begin laying out the new interior. This stage is always a challenge and fun.

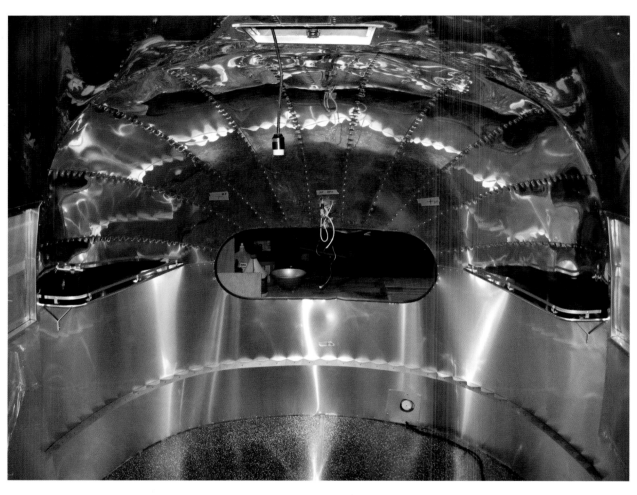

Tape is marking where the electric lies behind the walls with shelves installed over the bed. Aluminum perimeter supports being riveted to delineate the shape of the bed.

Squaring the two dividers that will support a deep drawer under the bed. There will be access to every open space beneath the bed for storage. They will also house speakers and a subwoofer for the sound system.

I liked the idea of having the front and rear interior aluminum end caps polished. But that effect is very powerful and I wanted to have contrasting wood tones. I sent Bob wood and stain samples and he chose walnut. The stain was a 50% cherry. This really added depth and warmth to the wood, especially when clear coats were applied. As with most of my trailers, I use aluminum edgings and extrusions. I like the contrast and its durability.

The layout of the trailer needed to be very precise due to space constraints. The bathroom had to be large enough to be practical, yet fit between a window and the galley.

Installation of the walnut bulkhead separating the bathroom from the galley.

We began with the dinette area in the final construction. There was going to be a lot of wiring routed through this area due to a humongous stereo system that I was installing. There are speakers in the front and rear with a massive 12" subwoofer under the bed. I wasn't sure how Bob was going to react when he sat on the bed and I turned up the volume.

Rear storage locker between the bed and bathroom with a pivoting 12v quartz light.

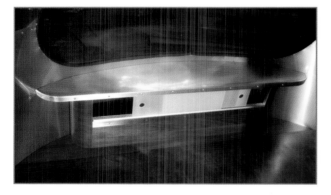

Storage cabinet with translucent doors: A 110v duplex is located inside the cabinet for a nightlight and a laptop.

Eclipse head unit and Eclipse amplifier which drives two pair of 2-way CDT speakers with 1" tweeters with an Alpine 12" subwoofer.

Installation of the rear portion of the sound system. This subwoofer could blow the blankets off the bed.

Behind both seat backs are storage lockers with pull-off covers. Under the seat [curb side] is a lift-off lid allowing the entire base for storage. The seat opposite contains the trailer's power supply and circuit breakers. Access is gained from under the seat cushions and from the front access panel. The dinette table lowers and cushions are arranged to form a twin-sized bed. The textiles came from the stock of fabrics that I've collected. In my opinion very few patterns and weaves fit vintage trailers and I'm always on the lookout for cool stuff.

Installation of the walnut dinette. Storage areas are behind the seat backs and under the right side seat base. The left side houses an electric systems panel.

Dinette converted to a bed. It's quite comfortable unless you're an NBA player.

I wanted to use something special in the galley area and chose corrugated copper as the backsplash. It was attached to the aluminum interior skin with copper rivets. I feel you need to be careful with copper. A little goes a long way. It can overwhelm its surroundings. It's like a rich chocolate cake. I clear coated the copper to bring down its shine and offer some resistance to abrasion.

The galley was framed in walnut plywood, although I used aluminum in the cabinet faces and also for the drawer faces. Kick plates are all removable for access to wiring and plumbing. A custom light fixture was fabricated and mounted under the polished aluminum overhead lockers.

Corrugated copper backsplash and vintage copper paper towel dispenser. Light fixture fabricated in the studio of perforated aluminum.

A view from the dinette.

At this point I was wishing that this trailer was going to stay with me.
It was difficult not to get attached to this trailer.

As I mentioned earlier, a window limited the bathroom placement, although it ended up being just the right size. I fabricated an aluminum base for the china toilet, which was riveted together for effect. I added a porthole style window in the bath door. I mention this because a funny thing happened. I was looking for something to trim the inner part of window with. A month or two earlier, I was making a riveted aluminum snare drum for Rikki Rocket of the band Poison [He's an Airstream fan]. I had a bent hardwood blank left over from a snare and it was the exact dimension of the inner circle in the door. It's cool when stuff like that happens.

The bed took up a sizable portion of the rear. I made the base in three sections. The two outboard sections have access to the base[s] under the mattress. In the center, supported by extra heavy-duty telescoping glides is a drawer that runs the depth of the bed. It's large enough for your mother in law to sleep in. Say goodnight and just close the drawer. Kidding. Sort of.

Installation of the china toilet and roof vent pipe.

Aluminum mounting base for the toilet, minus the side cover. Under the aluminum is a marine grade plywood base for strength.

Aluminum galley with perforated access panels below.

Finished bathroom with china toilet mounted on its aluminum base. A translucent window allows extra light. There is also a vintage light fixture. All dimensional wood is solid walnut.

On the curbside next to the bed we built a double wardrobe from floor to ceiling. Four solid walnut panel doors with heaps of room for clothes or whatever.

I situated the 2-way fridge on the left when entering the trailer. That allowed me to have a counter height surface abutting the wardrobe and it made a great location for a bar and a place to pour beverages. I have a collection of never-used vintage wall-mounted kitchen devices. I chose a terrific copper-plated can opener, an ice crusher, and a vintage bottle opener. I also had a cool bowling trophy from the '50s with a great patina. I attached the bowling guy next to a custom glass holder that I made. I also had some fun with the face of the fridge by riveting together three pieces of aluminum with a weathered Airstream exterior badge. The new refrigerators are so butt-ugly I'm always trying to find a way to enhance them.

A 42" deep drawer mounted on super heavy-duty extension glides. Walnut drawer face not shown.

The depth of the drawer is illustrated and its clearance of the bathroom door.

Finally, as you enter the trailer there is a shallow step. I wanted to have something notable as you step into the trailer. I inlaid "Airstream" in green linoleum into a black background. I thought it was a nice accent.

I really had a blast building this trailer. I felt that it was absolutely cool as hell. I'd like to have kept it. The total time was approximately five months in the studio. Upon completion I was anxious to have the trailer delivered to the factory and get Bob's reaction. I had been updating him with images while it was under construction but seeing it in person is a different story. He was blown away and that was a great feeling. He was also almost literally blown away when the stereo was turned up when he was sitting on the bed. Hoping to build him another in the future. Call me Bob.

A view of the completed cabinetry of the bathroom and bed area.

View of lower storage area of wardrobe. Shelf surfaces are extremely durable linoleum.

Double wardrobe with solid walnut doors.

Vintage Vornado® fan is a wonderful piece of industrial art and fits in perfectly.

Vintage NOS ice crusher and can opener. That opener would probably cost a hundred dollars today if it were remanufactured. What a shape.

View towards dinette.
On the right is a 2-way refrigerator.

A fun glass holder made in the studio. And the glasses are within easy reach of the bar area. Some might find that an important feature. Myself included.

Anchoring the left side of the glassware holder is the top of a vintage bowling trophy with a great patina. I think it's a great place to hang your keys.

View rearward across the bar of the finished interior.

The word "Airstream" in linoleum inlay seemed to be a fitting welcome to this trailer on the entry step.

We fabricated this simple aluminum holder for these spun aluminum salt and peppers.

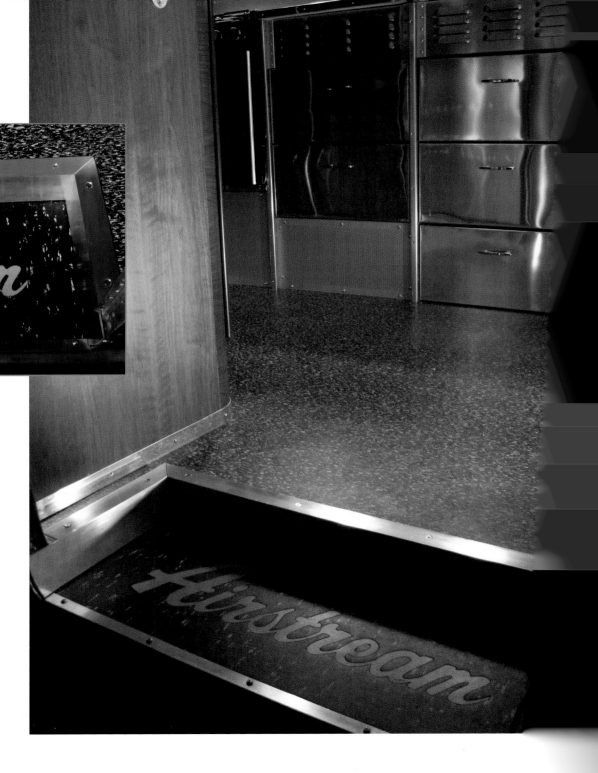

A view from the front highlighting the galley, fridge, and rear area.

Custom half-round sconce and fiberglass shades flanking the dinette.

Air inlet and outlet louvered panels fabricated for the Flying Cloud.

Flying Cloud build plate and my studio's aluminum signature badge.

CUSTOM BUILT FOR BOB WHEELER, CEO AIRSTREAM CO.

1950 Airstream Flying Cloud

DESIGNED AND FABRICATED BY DAVID WINICK

PRESENTED ON AUGUST, 2007 JACKSON CENTER, OHIO

Presentation plate riveted to the wall over the dinette.

Oval Beach, Grand Haven, Michigan.

Oval Beach, Grand Haven, Michigan.

Oval Beach, Grand Haven, Michigan.

Oval Beach, Grand Haven, Michigan.

Chapter Four:

1948
Wee Wind

This is my latest project and I feel that this is one of the best to date. I attempt to make each trailer better than the last and I incorporated many lessons from previous experience. We also incorporated advances in technology to assist in design and fabrication.

In the summer of 2008, a couple in a small town about 25 miles away contacted me. They sent an email and inquired if I was interested in purchasing a 1948 Airstream Wee Wind that they owned. Was I interested? Obviously they couldn't see the smile on my face on their computer monitor. I drove up to check out the trailer, and took lots of images. They were hot-rodders and used the trailer as a cool prop to tow behind their '32 Chevy coupe. The trailer was intact with about everything that it came with from the factory but had suffered a pretty amateurish 'restoration' at some point in its past. Structurally it was very straight and sound for a 60+-year-old trailer and we struck a deal.

This trailer is so small it's huggable. Very few Wee Winds exist and even fewer hit the open market for sale. My understanding is that there about a dozen in existence out of a production run of about sixty units from 1947-1949.

At the time I bought the Wee Wind I was art directing a feature film being shot in Grand Rapids but I was so eager to get started on the Wee Wind I began working on it along with my responsibilities on the film. My plan was to totally strip the trailer to its frame and store all the usable components until I could devote all my time to its rebuilding after we wrapped the film.

To offer a short background on the Wee Wind, one must take into account that the Airstream Company was in its infancy at the time and these trailers were totally hand-built. The little Wee Wind measures thirteen feet eight inches in the interior with an additional two feet to the coupler. This was one of the smallest of all Airstreams every produced. The title states, eleven hundred twenty pounds making it also one of the lightest. Unfortunately it also had the infamous pipe-frame chassis. This brainstorm consisted of a four-inch diameter thin-walled tube welded to a coupler, sixteen feet long, that ran the length of the trailer and tied in [sort of] to four pair of perpendicular aluminum outriggers. It sort of looks like a fish skeleton. For some reason someone thought that this was a good idea. I've always felt that the company must have made a good buy on surplus pipe and were trying to get rid of it by hiding it in trailer chassis. I don't know how many catastrophic frame failures these trailers suffered, but I'm sure there were plenty. The only points of attachment to the aluminum outriggers were small aluminum tabs screwed to the pipe. And to me, with what appears to be an

1948 Airstream Wee Wind at the Palazzolo Estate.

afterthought, a jumbo four-inch U-bolt at the front of the trailer sandwiching the pipe to the subfloor. This was the last line of defense to keep the pipe and trailer together as a happy couple. I wonder how many people had looked into their rear view mirrors only to find that the pipe had come sliding out like a Popsicle stick leaving the trailer behind. Oops. This design was changed very quickly to a ladder frame.

The 1948 Wee Wind, as found.

Cast copper logo still remained, as did most everything else.

Air-conditioner in the window is a nice touch.

The aluminum galley was lost over the years
and a crude one remained.

The original cabinetry remained and was pretty much unmolested.

This was going to be a major rebuild. The trailer needed to be totally disassembled and new parts fabricated. We had this trailer in so many pieces you could have put them in a box, stuck a postage stamp on it, and sent it through the mail.

Aside from its extreme light weight and diminutive length, one of the stellar features of this trailer is its beautiful form. The front and rear end are semi-circles. There are thirteen aluminum panels that make up the compound curves in the front and rear. The lips of each panel were hand-fed through an edge beader, giving the trailer a bit of an oriental feeling in the way that they overlap with the raised bead. I love that look. Rounding off the exterior is three automotive-style, double pane, sliding glass windows on the sides and two fixed matching oval windows in the front and rear end caps. An interesting addition was the original owner's name and social security number embossed on an aluminum tag screwed to the entry door. Oh, the good old days.

Please skip this section if details bore you senseless:

We began by securely raising and leveling the trailer on jack stands and employed overhead support with a padded lifting eye cabled to the shop's ceiling. We needed to keep the trailer square during disassembly, also ensuring that the trailer ribbing stayed in alignment. At this point we removed a million screws and dropped the belly pans. Next, we braced the aluminum cross members perpendicular with steel and securely clamped everything together. When we were confidant that the trailer wasn't going to collapse like a house of cards, the 4" main tube was slid out of the trailer and I began to remove the aluminum cross members one by one and replace them with identical pieces we fabricated. We used a heavier gage than stock for both the main tube and cross members.

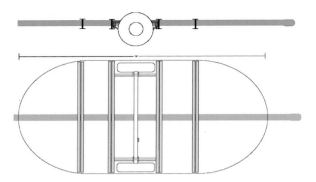

Original pipe frame chassis.

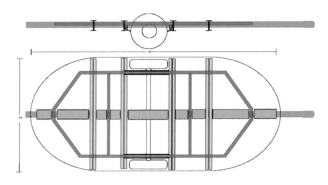

Modified chassis with the addition of a ladder-type frame.

The infamous pipe-frame chassis.

The axle and spindles were in good condition. Every other part of the running gear was replaced. In a jig that ensured that everything was square, we assembled the new springs and shackles and mounted the axle between a pair of aluminum cross members. When complete, we lifted the assembly onto a shop jack and positioned it under the trailer, raised and squared it to the newly replaced cross members. Squared and in alignment, it was then secured with temporary steel bracing and about every clamp I had in the shop.

It was now time to add steel to make the frame really structurally secure. Two-inch steel angle was added on both sides of the main tube crossing over the two steel U-channels supporting the springs and axle. The 2" angle was a perfect fit in the U-channel and when inserted formed a box and was welded in place giving the trailer the support it had needed for 60 years. The steel passing over and through notches in the aluminum was riveted with gussets. Since steel and aluminum should not be in direct contact, a protective coating was applied, keeping the surfaces from contacting.

When the frame was finished and the steel given a protective coat of paint, it was time to replicate the belly pans. There were four. In this model there is no pan in the axle area. These were duplicated exactly like the originals and riveted in place. The bottom portion of the trailer was now solid as a rock. It is so tight it could be used as a boat.

Next it was time to remove the aluminum outer skins. The front and rear panels had dents that weren't repairable. I decided to replace everything but the front and rear end caps, which were in beautiful condition. It wasn't possible to remove all the panels simultaneously as the trailer would have ceased to have any integrity and would collapse, so it was done in stages. Every section was braced prior to panel removal. We began at the rear and worked our way forward. It was easy and most of the time was spent riveting.

Fabrication of new jack and coupler.

One of the original belly pans being flattened to use as a pattern.

A completed belly pan ready to install.

Exact replacements
of these wheel-tubs
will be fabricated
from a heavier gage
galvanized steel.

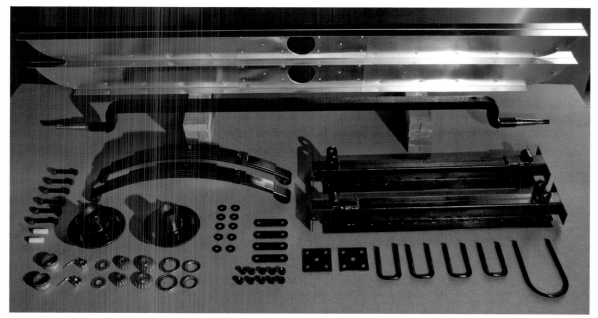

New aluminum frame members behind new
and refurbished suspension components.

Assembling the new
suspension components
prior to installation.

Positioning the suspension and raising it into place.

Squaring and aligning the suspension.

Fabricating and welding a new ladder frame.

Finished chassis with new wheel-tubs.

When we got to the entry door, it was re-skinned using the original rivet holes to maintain the same pattern. I soon discovered the frame was not in one piece but in several unconnected pieces—a surprise. So before taking the front and backside skins off, I needed to sister the parts and make it an integral frame, which was time consuming. I've no idea how this door was made in the factory. They must have been magicians.

The original interior was complete, with the exception of the galley. At some point it was removed and lost. Everything else was present, including sconces at the front and rear, drapery hardware, cabinetry, floor furnace, aluminum overhead locker with propane lamp, and box spring bed and sofa.

My first inclination was to refinish and keep the original interior, but there were a few things that changed my mind. On trailer curbside there was a tall wood veneered wardrobe with a small chest of drawers. Unfortunately the wardrobe was mounted over the window. This is how the trailer came from the factory. I think it's absurd and couldn't bring myself to cover half a window with a cabinet. So I began to re-think the interior. I decided to keep the basic floor plan and design a new interior. I have kept the original interior and it will accompany the trailer as a package. This trailer is so small that one must be modest in appointments and consider weight. My goal was to not have it weigh over thirteen hundred pounds. As it originally had an icebox, I made a concession to modern convenience and added a small two-way propane refrigerator. No electric water pump, but a marine hand-pump at the sink and a stainless sink plus cook top combo. Elegant and simple. There is not the slightest

possibility of having a toilet or shower in this rig. I suppose you could, but you would have to eliminate the bed, sitting area or the galley. Personally, I'm not too fond of sleeping three feet from a toilet anyway. I don't do it at home. At least not intentionally.

I wish to thank the companies and individuals who generously donated materials and services to assist in this project. I use Marmoleum® linoleum exclusively in my trailers and would like to thank Chris Cobb of the Forbo® Corporation, Steve Hingtgen of Vintage Trailer Supply®, and Mitzi Domyancic for the swell vintage awning. Also special thanks to Imtra® Marine Products, US distributor for Fynspray hand pumps and Progressive Dynamics® Inc. Their website and contact information can be found at the back of the book.

This was an exceptionally fun project. And also very time consuming. The Wee Wind is totally rebuilt from the axle up. Total time in the shop: four months. I would offer that it is better than new.

Exterior aluminum panel replacement begins.

Panel replacement was done in stages to protect
structural integrity.

At this point, front and rear panels have been replaced and we begin re-skinning the middle, one half at a time.

New chassis, new exterior panels, and belly-pans. Ready for the subfloor.

New floor awaiting installation.

Linoleum floor being cut to size.

Trailer is being wired and insulated after a new floor was installed.

Preparing to install all the rebuilt windows.

Thom Gohl [an excellent metal worker and overall good guy] lent a very welcome hand on this project as well as countless others. Thom is my son-in-law. He's worked with me for over 14 years on some very creative projects. We've also put in our fair share of rivets together.

Let's raise a glass.

Original owner's name and social security number embossed on an ID tag. A practice I wouldn't recommend today. The times were certainly different 60 years ago.

Thom and myself standing in front of the finest remaining Wee Wind.

One lucky E-bay find.
Listed in the wrong
category. Brand-new
in the original carton.
Extremely hard to find,
even in used condition.

Nice shots illustrating the new belly pans.

Front sofa with two hinged tables. Company logo inlaid in the surfaces.

Front sofa. Looks pretty inviting to me.

Rear bed. Measures out to be almost a double. Not bad for a 13' trailer.

View of the entry with both inlaid areas.

A mint vintage copper-based propane lamp.

Chapter Five:

1957 Airstream "18 Footer"

This is a good example of a trailer rebuilt on a modest budget. In 1957, several Airstream models went untagged, hence the name "Eighteen Footer."

Both Airstream factories in Ohio and California were producing them. This particular model was made in Ohio. The most obvious difference being varying well wheel shapes from both factories.

The trailer came by way of Canada to my shop. This model had a very plain original interior with a tiny bathroom that was originally on curbside adjacent to the entry door. The trailer's bathroom had been removed at some point during its long life. Only patches in the subfloor offered evidence of its existence.

My client wasn't so concerned about having a trailer that was a showboat on the exterior but rather their interest was having a wonderful, functional interior. Not everyone wants a polished trailer or has the budget. At first glance, the interior looked pretty solid, but on closer inspection revealed that it needed frame repair and an entire new floor. I wish I had a buck for every time I've heard, "My trailer has a solid floor, with no damage." I've yet to find a vintage trailer of any manufacture that didn't have damage. The plywood subfloor is the weak link in Airstreams and other brands. This trailer had extensive damage in the rear. It wasn't readily apparent until you removed the interior and chiseled off the old floor tiles exposing the subfloor [or what remained of it]. It also had been residence to enough critters to start a mobile zoo. This is not the glamour part of trailer work. You keep in mind that once everything is removed and the inner exterior skin power washed and disinfected, it's revived. The same goes for sandblasting and repainting the frame.

The next step was to remove two deteriorated steel frame members in the rear, fabricating and welding in new ones. A new subfloor was fitted and a floor of sheet Marmoleum® was installed. All the musty, moldy odors vanished with the old floor and insulation.

A 1957 Airstream "Eighteen Footer" as it arrived at my studio.

Pictures of the interior taken and sent to me by the owner. This is the dinette. Cannot be put into words. Yes it can. Butt-ugly.

Wardrobe and small chest of drawers, left of entry door.

An image of the galley. I couldn't wait to strip out this interior. It hurt my eyes.

A picture of the dinette taken from the entry.

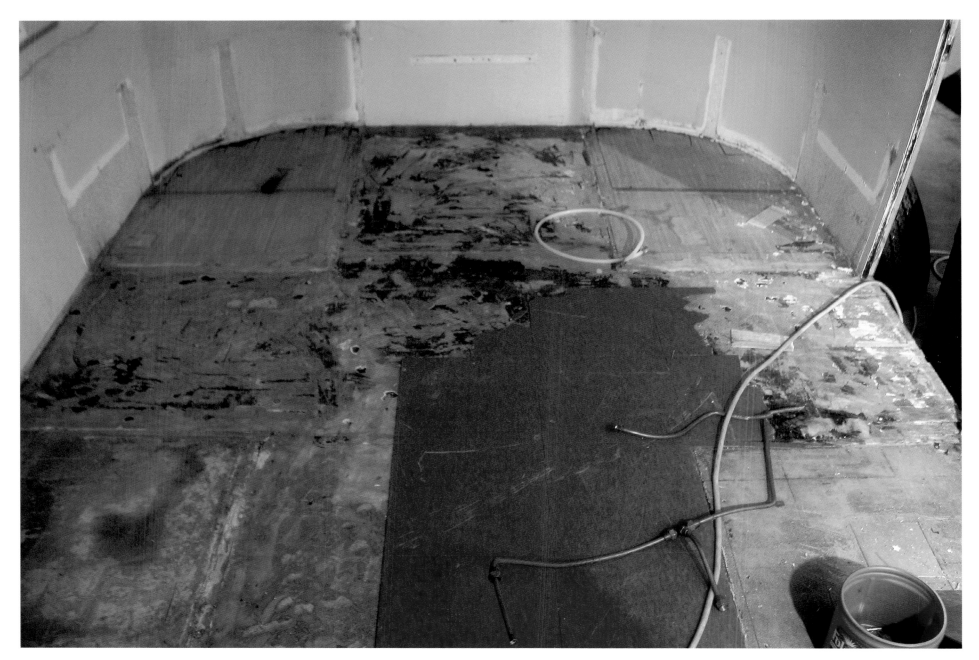

As usual, vintage trailers suffer from some form of floor damage. Either from a window or a vent being left open, or from defective plumbing. This one had serious damage in the rear. Plus two cross members that needed to be removed and new ones fabricated and welded in place.

124

Beginning to expose the floor damage.

The plywood was disintegrating under the old tile floor. The tile was the only thing holding it together. By the way, there were two tile floors, one laid over another.

This trailer should have been named "Mobile Mouse Motel." Once cleaned out of the former residents' homes, the insulation, wiring, and everything else was discarded. Now it was time to clean the hell out of it and remove the moldy odors once and for all.

The trailer interior smelled and looked new again and was ready for wiring, plumbing, and insulation. At this point, the front interior end-cap was removed in one piece. It was stripped of layers of old paint and then buffed to a mirror-shine and reinstalled.

New mill-finish aluminum interior panels were riveted in place and the upper ceiling panels were painted with an industrial coating.

With frame and walls exposed, the interior was power washed, disinfected, and the frame repainted. Also, any damage to the belly pan was repaired. No mouse was getting into this trailer again. Not on my watch.

Another shot of the interior while it's being stripped out.

I reused the original galley base cabinet after refinishing it. I also reused the birch storage locker above after removing several layers of paint. I was going to toss it before I found a safe way to remove the paint without damaging the thin veneer.

New cabinetry was built for the remainder of the trailer. I used Baltic Birch curved ply and sheet goods. I liked the natural tones of this wood. I also introduced some curves in the cabinets to give it a more of a vintage look.

All windows were resealed and gaskets replaced.

The front end cap after it was removed, stripped of several layers of paint, and polished. New aluminum sheet was installed everywhere else.

The entry door was disassembled and rebuilt.

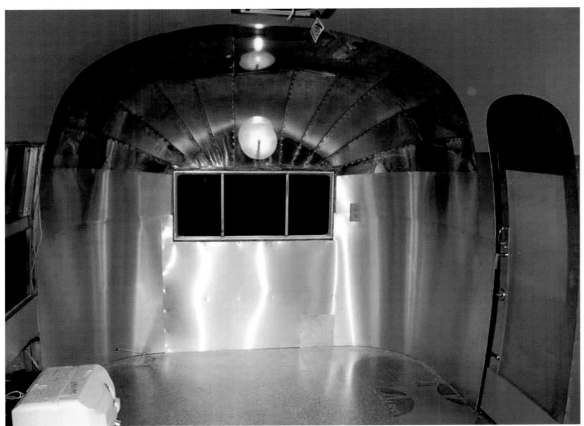

Another shot of the polished front end cap. At this point the trailer was ready for new cabinetry and components.

The dinette base cabinets have a lift off panel under the cushions for storage. The upholstery is a mix of new fabric with vintage bark cloth panel inserts with lots of storage accessible behind the back cushions. The water heater was hidden behind a false cabinet next to the dinette and can be used as additional seating at the dinette table. Like most trailers, the table lowers to convert into a bed.

Self-contained electrical service mounted on aluminum diamond plate box. 12v converter/charger manufactured by Progressive Dynamics, 110v service panel and deep cycle Optima marine battery [not shown].

Electrical center with battery, 12V converter, and main service panel. Assessable either by removable interior panel or exterior door.

Finished dinette with new cushions and upholstery.

Upholstery included new with vintage bark cloth panels.

New galley with refinished and new components.

Close up of galley base cabinet

The base of the rear bed was inset to offer more floor space and to further the open feeling of the trailer layout. Adjacent to the bed is a small chest of drawers and a tall wardrobe for clothing. Attached to the wardrobe is a fairly large cabinet with a counter top.

I felt that this trailer's finished interior was modest but had a warm, inviting feeling. I can easily imagine this trailer at a campground in a forest with the owners sitting around a flickering campfire ... *with the mice living in the forest where they belong.*

I stepped back the base of the bed to expose more floor and used curved plywood to soften the lines.

A view of the rear bed with removable cushions with storage underneath.

Completed dinette with vintage and new textiles.

Vintage lighting was rebuilt using NOS fiberglass shades.
I have a large collection of lighting components.

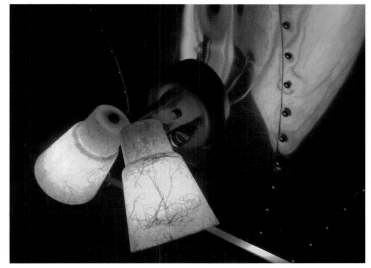

View towards the rear showing galley and bed.

A mixture of new and refinished original Birch cabinetry with a natural finish.

Another view of the wardrobe and a storage cabinet.

View from bed to front galley area.

Future Projects

Who would have thought that a hobby could turn out to be such a fun business? I've always endeavored to do work that was challenging and personally rewarding. And the most important component to me is being proud of what I've done. There is nothing more satisfying than doing your best. I've been fortunate to have so many fulfilling experiences. I feel that this effort is not popular anymore. Seems that the end goal is more important than the process of getting there. And *that's* the best part.

As of this writing, the studio has some great commissions that are well along in process, but not ready to include in this book.

A few weeks ago, Anthony Kiedas of the Red Hot Chili Peppers stopped in the studio unannounced and bought a 1958 Flying Cloud that we are now in the process of rebuilding for him. I'm very excited to be working on this project with him and it's going to be a fantastic rig.

We have many other projects lined up in the future and that will hopefully lead to an all new second edition.

Here's to rebuilding Americana, one rivet at a time.

Afterword

Cavalcade: a dramatic sequence, in the sense that it covers a period of time from my birth until today. And it also covers the over 75 years of rich Airstream history.

Airstream has always been part of this progression through my life. Wally Byam, my first cousin once removed, founded Airstream. My mother, Helen Byam Schwamborn, was put in charge of fostering and growing the Wally Byam Caravan Club. The central image of my life and that of thousands of other people is the Airstream trailer. It is the iconic trailer that enjoys worldwide recognition.

For many years I have been on a hiatus from the Airstream World, but not from the Airstream family. This year I have spent time with several units of the Wally Byam Caravan club. I've been to San Antonio, TX, Cottonwood, AZ, Washington, DC, Pittsburgh, PA, Madison, WI, and look forward to visiting Missouri and Ohio later this year.

Many of the Airstreamers I have met with or traveled with are members of the VAC [Vintage Airstream Club, a sub-unit of the WBCCI] who take great pride in their vintage Airstreams.

There is always frequent talk about the new vintage trailer to be purchased. Someone's new find or did you see so-and-sos restored '63 Overlander? Someone was very complimentary about a recently restored Airstream. Yea, it was a 'Winick'.

What is a 'Winick'?

In Madison, WI, at the 2009 International Rally I met 'The Winick'. That is David Winick. David is a legend in the Airstream world. He has done artistic, yet creative design work in bringing vintage Airstreams to new life, long after their original factory delivery.

David is the real thing. You really need to sit down and talk with him to find his passion in giving a second life to older Airstreams. He's smart, dedicated, and fun to talk with about his world and the Airstream world.

I also had learned that David designed Airstream's 75th Anniversary model. I heard compliments from many Airstreamers, but I had never seen the Winick Signature Model Bambi. I recently went to David's website and went through a series of photographs. The choice of colors, fabrics, woods, cabinetry, and spirit are evident of the rich Airstream history. But the kudos go to David's blending of the history with today's technology that Airstream puts into their newer models.

I believe Wally Byam would have hired David to do design work for the company.

It was nice meeting you David. Keep up the excellent work.

Dale "Pee Wee" Schwamborn

Resources

Winick Airstreams: www.winickairstreams.com

Manufacturers

Airstream Corporation: www.airstream.com

Clubs

Airstream: www.vintageairstreamclub.net
Tin Can Tourists: www.tincantourists.com
Wally Byam Caravan Club: www.wbcci.org

Supplies and Materials

Forbo Group: www.forbo.com
Imtra Marine Products: www.imtra.com
Vintage Trailer Supply: www.vintagetrailersup-
    ply.com
Progressive Dynamics Inc.: www.progressivedyn.
    com
Marti Domyancic (vintage awnings): domy@
    sbcglobal.net
Moonshine Lamp and Shade: www.moonshine-
    shades.com

Creative

Rebecca Gohl: www.rebeccagohl.com
Gregg Palazzolo, Palazzolo Design Studio: www.
    palazzolodesign.com